I0460806

John Gillette's writings flow from a lifetime of experience. It is one thing to write out of a knowledge based on research. It is an entirely different thing to write out of a depth of life experience. John has both. As a pastor who has cared for the needs of a congregation, as a husband who has experienced the tragic loss of a wife, and as a child of God who has walked through the joys and pain of following the Lord, John has so much to offer in this series. From the opening pages, through to the very end, you will be blessed by the insights, loving tone and encouragement you receive from this series. God has used John greatly in ministry and will continue to use him through this life-giving series.

—*Josh Mateer, D. Min.*

True, illustrative, practical stories are like windows that unlock Bible truths and promises. Along with a masterfully orchestrated short stories should come the truth that God's Word and love has been experienced by His servants as they partner with Him in the work of rebuilding the Kingdom. A gifted teacher, Dr. Gillette lives an ordinary life abiding in Christ and being an obedient servant of the Lord. As he sees God working in his life, and in the lives of those to whom he ministers, his faith is refreshed and he is encouraged to press on through life's uncertainties.

Only a lifetime dedicated to nurturing, ministering, teaching, and keen insight through the power of the Holy Spirit, can produce such poignant stories that teach and challenge.

—*Mulonge M. Kalumbula, Ph.D.*

John's books give us hope and light. He reminds us that through Jesus we are never alone. I have certainly needed that reminder in my life and in my practice. In holding a patient's hand, and helping them through a condition or disease, reminding them that they are never alone has become the greatest gift of health care.

—*Linda M. Kunce, D.C.*

The series reminds me that Jesus knows what it's like to live in a human body. I have received Jesus and His forgiveness, but as the book suggests, I also have the power from the Holy Spirit. His books have encouraged me to gain courage through prayer and confidence in Jesus to meet my needs. John's honesty is very special to read as he reflects on his own life and struggles. I like his explanation that "the soul is where the emotions are and the mind is where the thinking takes place". It's been good for me to read that God works through weakness, and learn that John found God with him in the middle of the struggles.

—*Arvid W. Vandyke, Ed.D.*

Discovering God's Counsel is a book full of great spiritual truths from someone who has developed a very close and deep relationship with Jesus through his life. John provides a meaningful and inspirational testimony, with examples from his own experiences, of how relying on God's Word and promises can give you the power, hope, and peace you need to overcome life's struggles and challenges. The Scriptures he chose in his book were on point and helpful. It was an enjoyable and wonderful read.

—*Thoa Reyna, J.D.*

John has written a user-friendly and practical series for anyone desiring to live beyond the superficial and venture into the supernatural. The world needs this *Pastoral Health Care Series*. Pastors and followers of Jesus need the insights from John's lifetime experience of walking with God and caring for His people through the power of the Holy Spirit. John has brilliantly show that God is enough, God's love is real, God's counsel is enduring, and God reigns supremely. This important series will serve both the church and the world for many years to come.

—*Kizombo Kalumbula, Jr., Ph.D.*

John Gillette's inspirational book *Glorify God* is a fantastic reminder of how I should approach each day and how blessed I am. It is so easy to get caught up in the hustle and bustle of today's lifestyle and forget what is really important. John's encouraging words are a great reminder of how we all should live each day. I have a great foundation of faith nut John's book helps me to remember what is important and allows me to reflect on the wonderful things I have and to be gracious to God for those blessings.

— *Tammy Thelen, Au.D., CCC-A*

Note from the Author

I believe in God's sovereignty and compassion. I am learning to let go of self and to hold onto someone that can do whatever he pleases. Sometimes life is cruel, sometimes it is full of suffering, physically and psychologically. A spiritual solution to meet difficult trials has become my goal. God's Word carries with it no uncertainties. I want it to saturate my mind and heart..

The *Pastoral Health Care Series* and *Divine Dialogue Series* was created through unexpected heart disease (open heart surgery), cancer (medication and surgery), a stroke and major head injury after a car accident that also resulted in the death of my wife.

It is helping me to develop and adequate level to supernatural, psychological and physical adjustments. It may help you as well. It has brought me security.

—*John F. Gillette, D.S.M., D.Min*

DISCOVERING

GOD'S

Supernatural
Activities

DISCOVERING
GOD'S
Supernatural
Activities

*Why Do I Believe
in Jesus Christ?*

JOHN F. GILLETTE

Chapbook Press

Schuler Books

2660 28th Street SE

Grand Rapids MI 49512

www.schulerbooks.com/chapbook-press

Fantastic Favorites Book Series Part One

Discovering God's Supernatural Activities: Why Do I Believe in Jesus Christ?

Copyright ©2023 — John F. Gillette. All rights reserved. Published 2023.

Printed at Schuler Books, Chapbook Press, Grand Rapids, Michigan, in the United States of America.

Distribution contact:at jjgillette@comcast.net.

ISBN 13: 9781957169392

Library of Congress Control Number: 2023903873

Cover photo: Paige Weber/Unsplash
Cover Design: Frank Gutbrod Graphic Design

Printed in the United States of America

Books by John Gillette:

Pastoral Health Care

Discovering God's Sufficiency
Going Beyond Ourselves and Experiencing the Supernatural
Part One

Discovering God's Love
Confirming God's Love Through the Evidence of Historical Facts
Part Two

Discovering God's Counsel
Applying His Spiritual Solution to Meet Difficult Trials
Part Three

Discovering God's Kingdom
Finding a Way to Understand Ourselves in a Complex World
Part Four

Discovering God's Heart
Finding God's Heart Pulse is Our Daily Challenge
Part Five

Divine Dialogue

Glorify God
Christianity is a Divine Vitality
Part One

Dynamic Doer
Biblical Christianity is Jesus Christ
Part Two

Satisfying Strength
Biblical Meditation Works — Allow Psalms to Sweep You into All Directions
Part Three

Disciplining Dynamics
Christian Counseling Teaching Tools
Part Four

Celebrate Christ
Above All Christ
Part Five

Fantastic Favorites

Discovering God's Presence
A Pastoral Health Devotional
Part One

Discovering God's Favor
A Triplet's Faith Journey
Part Two

Discovering God's Supernatural Activities
Why Do I Believe in Jesus Christ?
Part Three

Joy and John Gillette

It is with great affection that I dedicate this book series to my wife Joy, who radiated God's grace. We wrote the Pastoral Healthcare Series together. Applying God's spiritual solutions to meet us in difficult trials has become even more practical in my life with the recent death of my dear wife, Joy.

This book has been reproduced in her memory while the content is the same, my dedication has become more personal than ever before. The separation is painful, but as I gather my suffering and feelings of incompleteness, I will succeed with God's peace and presence. The guidelines of this book have brought blessing to our life together. We have pursued them with great persistence. I am assured she is in God's presence rejoicing and at peace. I will be with her to experience God's eternal presence someday as well. " . . . Blessed are they who put their trust in him." (Psalm 2:12)

*I am thankful and appreciate
my Editorial Advisor, Miriam Stuart,
for her professionalism, knowledge,
insight, and sensitivity.*

Table of Contents

Introduction

So much knowledge is gained by asking questions. There are many important questions that need to be answered in our lifetime. Where do I come from? Why am I here? Where am I going? The answer to these questions, and numerous others, can be solved by answering this question: Why do I believe in Jesus Christ?

Why do you believe in Jesus Christ is a question I have been asked quite often. I have given many Biblical answers. They concern my spirit, soul, and body. *Man is a spirit* because he is dependent on God. This is the nucleus of life. It is an in-breathing of God that caused an endless life not subject to death (Genesis 2:9). *Man is a soul* because he has the likeness of God (Genesis 1:26-27). He has personality, individuality, intellect (mind), understanding, sensibility, emotion, and will (decision). *Man is a body.* He possesses flesh, bone, nerves, brain, blood, and vital organs.

A believer has been regenerated by Jesus. He is my substitute on the cross. He is my Sovereign God. He is my salvation. *Invitation* is God's action on my being. *Security* is knowing my eternal future is sealed by His Spirit. *Perspective* is God's point of view giving me understanding. *Supernatural events* have taken place to produce faith. *Passion* from God has produced an urgent need to believe. *Justification* is God's legal leadership to cause a way to be redeemed. The *presence of God* is real and absolute. *Resurrection* is God's final proof for confidence. *Cleansing* is the new birth and *action* is the response to faith. Let these thoughts motivate your spirit to make a decision to believe.

I have *submitted* my life to Jesus through confession of faith in who He is and what He has done for me. His *supernatural* nature has given me conviction and confidence. I have assurance of the facts and have consecrated my life in *service.*

ONE

Supernatural Invitation

The Bible says, "All that the Father giveth me shall come to me."

ROMANS 8:29-30

The invitation is open to you, "Come unto me" (Matthew 11: 28-30). I am grateful for my decision. Have you read Jesus' words, "Come unto me" in Matthew 11:28-30? Have you heard his sweet, deep, sensitive, authentic, bold, eternal, changing words?

"Come unto me" is an open invitation. Let's discover what Jesus means with such awesome words. We will start with a little background. The Gospel according to Matthew gives a view of the life of Jesus. Most likely, the early accounts were passed on verbally in the Aramaic language and then recorded in Greek manuscripts dating from A.D. 60 to A.D. 90. Matthew emphasizes the Old Testament preparation for the gospel and makes it an ideal "bridge" from the Old and New Testament. Matthew, the Hebrew tax collector, writes for the Hebrew mind. He tells us that Jesus is the Messiah foretold by Old Testament prophets. He starts with the genealogy of Jesus. The coming of Christ to the earth has been anticipated from the beginning. In the early days of human history, God has chosen one family line, that of Abraham, and later on another family in Abraham's line, that of David, to be the family through which His Son would make entrance into the world.

Miracles, lessons learned and many activities have already taken place, but now we have come to Matthew 11:28-30 to think about Jesus' sweet words "come unto me." The purpose of the gospel is to present the good news of the Redeemer-Savior. Jesus is the Messiah of Israel, the Son of God, and the Savior of the world.

The words "come unto me" are life changing words which can't be heard by our sinful, rebellious, and stubborn minds without a sovereignly bestowed spiritual awakening. We have a free offer to all in verses 28-30 and a divine initiative in verse 27. I'm so glad that the Holy Spirit convicts us and that the sovereign work of God is at hand so we can trust our spirit, soul, and body to Jesus Christ. Authority and confidence are found in verse 27. "All things are delivered unto me of my father; and no man knoweth any man the Father, save the Son, and he to whom so ever the Son will reveal him." Jesus is the way initiated by the Father. "My Father" reveals Jesus' absolute equality, He is the "only begotten Son." Personal knowledge of the Father through the Son with the assistance of the Holy Spirit will develop assurance and authority in living. How does genuine conversion take place? The songwriter says, "only trust Him" and the text continues with the answer.

"All ye that labor and are heavy laden" are words that describe our condition. If we are going to hear God's call through Jesus, we have to be in a condition of humility. The labor and burden have brought us to exhaustion and just plain sweat. We have to lay our load at Jesus' feet. Trying to save ourselves will not work. Doing all the good works as well as a guilty conscience will not do it, but a broken heart realizing total dependence is necessary. We will hear His voice, "come unto me" when we recognize our sinful condition. In the present condition we don't measure up to God's standards.

In my childhood, I responded to Jesus. I had been singing with my sisters at a Bible conference. On the way home, our mother asked if we would like to ask Jesus into our hearts. We knew the gospel story. Because of sin, we were separated from God (Romans 3:23), and the penalty for sin is death (Romans 6:23). Thankfully that penalty for sin was paid by Jesus Christ (Romans 5:8). If we repent of the sin — acknowledge need — then confess and trust Jesus as Lord and Savior — accept Jesus — we will be saved (Romans 10:9). Right there in the car on the side of the road, I was "born of God" and a second birth — spiritual — took place (I John 5:11-12). This birth is clearly stated in John 3:8, "The wind bloweth where it listeth, and thou hearest the sound thereof, but cannot tell whence it cometh, and whither it goeth: so is everyone that is born of the Spirit." The wind, which is the same word used for Spirit, cannot be seen or explained. The word can only be heard or observed in relation to its effect. The new birth is spiritual and invisible. One can only observe the results. It's a decision of faith based upon facts. The first element in trusting Jesus is total dependency.

"And I will give you rest . . . ye shall find rest unto your souls" is a powerful claim. It's not only a dependent heart that is necessary but the discovery of divine truth found in Jesus Christ who provides the rest for our souls. Liberation is given through Jesus because of who He is. In the Gospel of John, Jesus is revealed as the eternal, pre-existing Son of God who became man in order to reveal the Father and bring eternal life through His death and resurrection.

John says: "Now Jesus did many other signs in the presence of his disciples, which are not written in this book; but these are written that you may believe that Jesus is the Christ, the Son of God, and that believing you may have life in his name" (John 20:30-31).

Jesus is God. "In the beginning was the Word, and the Word was with God, and the Word was God. He was in the beginning with God" (John 1:1). John 1:14 says that "the Word became flesh." The key term, 'Word', refers to Jesus. Jesus is fully God. These phrases are vital to understand. "In the beginning" refers to eternity past. It goes beyond His earthly life, beyond even the beginning of Creation. "With God," refers to an affirmation of Christ's separate personality. There is diversity within the Godhead. "And God was the Word," refers to the fact that Jesus is fully divine in all respects. We can trust Jesus because He is God. He has the authority and power to redeem us and bring us into His family.

"Take my yoke upon you and learn of me; for I am meek and lowly in heart," is a text full of challenges and life changing possibilities. We must turn around in our thinking. We must turn to Jesus and repent. Our way to acceptance and forgiveness are not acceptable. A complete turnaround and a full change of direction is necessary. We have come to the end of our resources. As we learn of Him, we discover our self-regulations. Work-based convictions will not be sufficient. He is gentle and tender and is calling us to Himself. As we turn from our sin and replace it with faith, a new direction takes place. This is not an intellectual exercise but a whole heart change.

"For my yoke is easy and my burden is light," reminds us that salvation in Jesus Christ includes an invitation to surrender. If we want His saving rest, we must take His yoke. The yoke is a symbol of submission. It is used by the master to direct us. Discipline is a natural part of genuine conversion. The yoke is submission to Christ and is not grievous. It is joyous.

My childhood song to live by tells it all, "I have been chosen by the Father, purchased by the

Son, and sealed by the Spirit, I'm his very own" (Ephesians 1). As a child, I did not understand everything and even now I still do not. His grace is amazing and His sovereignty is above us. All He wants me to do is take Him at His word. He said, "By one man (Adam), sin entered into the world and death by sin, and so death passed upon all men for all have sinned" (Romans 5:12). "Behold I was shaped in iniquity" (Psalm 51:5). I do not like reading these words, but God said it and I have to accept it. I have discovered that "Ye have chosen me" (John 15:16). "It is God who worketh in you both to will and to do of his good pleasure" (Philippians 2:13). He is drawing me to Himself (John 6:44). He has saved me and called me according to His own purpose and grace (II Timothy 1:9).

I am so glad that I was taught by my parents in the early years that "God commendeth his love toward us in that while we were yet sinners, Christ died for us" (Romans 5:8). As I have grown in Jesus Christ, I have seen His sovereign grace at work. He saved me not by works of righteousness that I have done, but according to His mercy by the working of regeneration and renewing of the Holy Spirit (Titus 3:5).

I live every day knowing "in whom I have believed and am persuaded that he is able to keep that which I have committed unto him against that day" (II Timothy 1:12). Salvation is of the Lord. I am safe because the Father has chosen me, the Son has purchased me and the Holy Spirit has sealed me. Salvation occurs when God changes the heart and unbelievers turn from sin to Christ (Colossians 1:13). Faith is the process for Jesus to enter the heart and dwell there (Ephesians 3:17). Praise the Lord! As I learn to follow Jesus, life will become a celebration because it involves His supernatural power.

Personal Response

TWO

Supernatural Security

The Bible says, "I have written unto you
that believe . . . that ye may know."

JOHN 1:12-13

Learning to live every moment in God's presence requires a personal relationship. My confidence is secure because I am assured of my relationship with Christ.

• Salvation is assured through God's Word (I John 5:11, 12).

"And this is the record, that God hath given to us eternal life and this life is in his Son. He that hath the Son hath life and he that hath not the Son of God hath not life. These things have I written unto you that believe on the name of the Son of God; that ye may know . . ."

- Salvation is assured through God's authority (John 1:12, 13).

  "But as many as received him, to them gave he power to become the Sons of God, even to them that believe on his name; which were born, not of blood, nor of the will of the flesh, nor of the will of man, but of God."

- Salvation is assured through God's security (John 10:27-30).

  "My sheep hear my voice and I know them, and they follow me: And I give unto them eternal life, and they shall never perish, neither shall any man pluck them out of my hand. My Father, which gave them to me, is greater than all, and no man is able to pluck them out of my Father's hand — I and my Father are one."

- Salvation is assured through God's grace (Ephesians 2:8-9).

  "For by grace are ye saved through faith, and that not of yourselves; it is the gift of God, not of works, lest any man should boast."

- Salvation is assured through God's justice (I Peter 3:18).

  "For Christ also hath once suffered for sins, the just for the unjust, that he might bring us to God, being put to death in the flesh but quickened by the Spirit."

- Salvation is assured through God's love (Romans 5:8).

  "But God commendeth his love toward us, in that while we were yet sinners, Christ died for us."

- Salvation is assured through God's transformation (II Corinthians 5:17).

  "Therefore if any man be in Christ, he is a new creature: old things are passed away and behold all things are become new."

God's presence involves a relationship that is secure.

Personal Response

THREE

Supernatural Perspective

The Bible says, "The spirit giveth life."
II CORINTHIANS 3:6

Sometimes life is cruel and full of suffering, physically and psychologically. Sometimes our expectations for life fail, there is little meaning to life, there is desperation and despair, or there is just a falling out in the realities of life. The Word carries with it no uncertainties. I can be sure of the faithfulness of God in fulfilling His promises. With hope, I have conviction and assurance. I want to become contagious with encouragement and endurance that springs from hope.

Those with difficult and long-standing problems or are misled in regard to their problems need hope. Those who are harassed by fear, have dashed hopes, or have failed often need hope. People who have experienced dramatic life changes, fallen into depression, or suffered life-shattering experience need hope.

When I find myself searching for help, I find it in the hope that I have in Jesus. I have learned through Psalm 39:1-13 that my innermost thoughts toward the wicked should be confident and not complaining. I should be watchful of what I say (v.1-2). My innermost thoughts toward God should be honest and not with a bitter attitude. I must share my anguish and pain with God (v.3-4). When I am searching for hope, my innermost thoughts toward myself should not be deceiving. I have to learn God's perspective on life (v.5-6). *My innermost thoughts toward deliverance should be Scripture-directed (v.7-13).* I have learned that in despair, I can experience confidence (v.7), in confession I can be released (v.8), and that correction is needed sometimes (v.9-11). I have been comforted (v.12-13).

I am discovering with excitement that in Jesus Christ's name, I can live with hope and obtain the help I need. He is worth believing. There is no one whose understanding of life has come close to His. Jesus is in the life changing business. All kinds of people have come to Him: the messed-up, sick, injured, forgotten, and despised. Even the satisfied, admired, worthy and religious people. I have come to Him. Jesus has been changing lives for two thousand years. I am learning to leap out of my comfort zone into faith. I realized that there must be less of me and more of Him. Not only do I have to let go of myself and replace myself with Him, I also have to learn to wait. This is the in-between period. When I hold onto His promise, "My hope is in Jesus . . . hear my prayer, O Lord, listen to my cry for help" (Psalm 39:7,12). I know victory will come because He keeps to His word. Some adjustments have to be made during the waiting time until victory. As I apply the attributes of God to the names given to Jesus, I will be given God's perspective.

His name is Wonderful (Isaiah 9:6). I believe in an awesome God. He can make my life wonderful because He is wonderful. My first adjustment in obtaining help is believing that He is awesome. Wonderful things have happened, are happening, and will continue to happen. It all starts with experiencing forgiveness of sin and the invasion of a whole new life. "Christ liveth in me" (Galatians 2:20). Believing in Jesus is required (Acts 16:31). He wants intimate fellowship. "I count all things to be a loss in view of the surpassing value of knowing Christ Jesus my Lord" (Philippians 3:7-8). Knowing God is the most important thing I can accomplish. My goal is to know Him so well that I can confidently say, "I have received a spirit of adoption as sons by which I cry, 'Abba! Father!'" The word 'Abba' is equivalent to 'Daddy'. It is a term of respect and endearment.

As a continuation of this first adjustment, I can better understand how I am to live by truly knowing God. As I contemplate God's attributes through His names, I have been promised strength, encouragement, and help. I know God loves me. God is love and the one who abides in love abides in God and God abides in Him (I John 4:16). I am surrounded with His infinite person, power, and glory (John 14:20). "And I will pray the Father, and He shall give you another Comforter, that He may abide with you forever . . . I am in my Father, and ye in me, and I in you" (v.16, 20). He says, "I am in you." He is more than me, He is *in* me. He also supplies in Himself all that any soul will ever need in time or for eternity. The union I have 'in Christ' is beyond my comprehension. The oneness that I have with Jesus means many things (John 17:20-23). My emphasis here is fellowship. It is awesome to say that I have an everlasting companionship with Him. In the place we live, He abides. I am looking for the eternal security which starts here and now as I draw near to Him. "To be in Christ" refers to my position with or my union to Christ. In believing, I have that relationship and possession of the divine. I am safe in His hands because I am associated with the Creator-Redeemer God. ***"Christ in me" refers to transformation power.***

His name is Counselor. I believe in an all-knowing God. He is my counselor. He knows everything. "Who has directed the Spirit of the Lord or as His counselor has informed Him? With whom did He consult and gave Him understanding? And who taught Him in the path of justice and taught Him knowledge, and informed Him of the way of understanding?" (Isaiah 40:13-14). God knows what He knows simply because He knows it. He did not learn it. The second adjustment is to accept His counsel. He is qualified to counsel me. He is eternal God in whom "dwelleth all the fullness of the Godhead bodily" (Colossians 2:9). Jesus Christ was a part of the eternal counsel of creation. He was there when the Father said, "Let us make man." He understands me because He became man. He is able to enter into the experiences that perplex and burden me. He knows my heart and mind. He is able to help me understand myself. I have to let go of myself and let Him take over. I must learn to sit back and watch Him work. He knows my feelings, desires, personality, and disease. He has known everything from the beginning (Acts 15:18). Nothing can escape His all-encompassing knowledge. I have learned that God permits trials for reasons we may or may not understand, but He is able to bring good out of the worst circumstances. I am able to have confidence because He knows all the possibilities. He is personal. The Bible says, "O Lord, thou hast searched me and known me" (Psalm 139:1-2). He knows my thought process (Ezekiel 11:5). God is concerned about the details; He knows everything going on behind the scenes (Job 23:10).

His name is Mighty God. I believe in a powerful God. Jesus is God Himself. There is nothing God cannot do. His unlimited power will reflect His divine glory and accomplish His sovereign will. "Power belongs to God" (Psalm 62:11). He is able to "call into being that which does not exist" (Romans 4:17). "He spoke and it was done" (Psalm 33:6). "Nothing is impossible with God" (Luke 1:37). The Scripture says, "Thou hast formed my inward parts . . . I am fearfully and wonderfully made" (Psalm 139:13-14). God's power is very personal. "Thy will be done" (Matthew 5) is my prayer. He is able to deliver (Daniel 3:17). He is able to keep me standing in His presence (Jude 24). He says to "be strong in the Lord and in the strength of His might" (Ephesians 6:10). The third adjustment for change is embracing the fact that He is "Mighty God." He is called "Immanuel" which means 'God with us.' I have to understand His claims and accept His deity. With that response, I am strengthened with all might. He takes care of the demands of life. No matter what the problem, He has the power to meet it, handle it, solve it, and use it for my good and for His glory.

His name is Everlasting Father. I believe in a sovereign God. He is the originator of eternity. I live in a new dimension of life. God has absolute rule and control over all His creation. God rules absolutely over the affairs of men. God can do whatever He wants simply because it is all His. "The earth is the Lord's and all it contains, the world, and those who dwell in it" (Psalm 24:1).

Everything that occurs does so under the hand of a sovereign God. The fourth adjustment for change is reveling in His name, the everlasting Father. God has created me for eternity and Jesus Christ came to earth to reveal eternity (I John 1:1, 2). There is more to life than what my senses reveal. In trusting Jesus, I am able to meet every detail of life with confidence. I am safe in Jesus because of who He is. I exist for Him. I can live in confidence because Jesus provides strength. There are no chance happenings. Whatever happens, it will bring good (Psalm 8:28). He has the whole picture. I can trust in Jesus and He is able to guard what I have entrusted to Him (2 Timothy 1:12).

His name is Prince of Peace. I believe in an intimate God. The fifth adjustment for change is peace. When I accomplish the alignment process through His grace, I will experience peace. Do not try to change the circumstances but change in character. In reality, peace does not come from the outside in, but from the inside out. I am learning that my testing, trials, and temptations can become a win-win situation. I must learn to let go of self. I must learn to make the adjustments. I must learn to practice victory in peace. He is free from the limitations of space. He is everywhere present. He is in me (I John 4:4). I believe in an awesome God because He is wonderful in all His acts. He wants fellowship with me. I believe in an all-knowing God because He provides wise counsel. He has all knowledge. He knows my inner needs. I believe in a powerful God because there is nothing He cannot do. He is in control. When I reflect upon these facts and allow them to penetrate my spirit, soul, and body, I am able to face today.

As I repeat the names of Jesus with a sincere heart and allow the Holy Spirit to enable me, I will be encouraged. This is a starting point. Authentic transformation takes time because it is a process. It is not a formula to follow; it is not a list of basic principles to apply. It is not a mechanical determination. It is faith working in me through the Holy Spirit's guidance and power. "May the God of hope fill you with all joy and peace as you trust in him, so that you may overflow with hope by the power of the Holy Spirit" (Romans 15:13).

The promise of help is provided through Jesus. I am thankful for the Lord's presence. This chapter was written when I started a new journey in my life. I am facing a fearful, dreadful uncertainty in my health. The biopsy has returned with a positive result. Cancer is the disease. I was told that my cancer is the second top killer of man. That information was really discouraging. I am waiting for the details and what treatment options I have. I do not like the side effects of any of them. I still need to know the facts. The initial shock has worn off. My family is very supportive. I know their prayers and spiritual perspective will continue to be helpful.

My daughter shared a prayer and Psalm 91:11, which says, "He who dwells in the shelter of the Most High will rest in the shadow of the Almighty." She has started a network of prayer support. My son immediately gave me a verse from Hosea 6:3, "Let us acknowledge the Lord

. . . as surely as the sun rises He will appear . . . He will come to us." He has also set up a network of prayer warriors. I am so pleased that they have accepted this challenge in the way that they have. They know what works and what pleases God. Without them knowing it, both Bible references reinforce the verse the Holy Spirit gave to me and my wife, James 4:8, "Draw near to God and He will draw near to you." My dark thoughts have turned to the light because Jesus is wonderful. My folly has turned to wise thinking because Jesus is my counselor. Losing heart has changed to a conquering spirit because Jesus is my mighty God. I have been drawing closer to my everlasting Father who holds eternity in His hands. When I think of these names of Jesus, peace from the Prince of Peace has entered my spirit. "Jesus is the sweetest name I know and He's just the same as His lovely name, and that's the reason why I love Him so, O Jesus is the sweetest name I know."

Personal Response

Supernatural Events

*The Bible says, ". . . the beginning of
miracles and the disciples believed."*

JOHN 2:4

Supernatural events of Jesus Christ give evidence that belief and faith count. Memorize John 2:11. "This beginning of miracles did Jesus in Cana of Galilee and manifested his glory and his disciples believed on him." God exists in Jesus Christ. Miracles are a part of the historical evidence. Read the first gospels with an open heart and the Holy Spirit will give you understanding.

Meditate on the supernatural activity of Jesus Christ. They will produce motivation that belief and faith work. The miracles represent relationship building, personal need, supernatural touch, and conviction to follow Christ. Let's look at each miracle and ponder over it. Look at your personal life and see if miracles are happening today.

Turn Water into Wine (John 2:1-11)

A small-town pastor receives a gracious gift: a cow and freezer from a farmer in town. It was a necessary need.

Orders the Wind and the Waves (Mark 4:35-41)

A music minister was forced to leave church and drive home through a tornado storm. The car shook; it was dangerous, but Christ calmed the wind.

Walk on Water (Matt 19:22-33)

A young pastor was called to a teenager suicide event. She was hanging from a tree. The family needed comfort and understanding. Christ brought peace in the bad situation.

Raises Lazarus to Life (John 11:17-44)

A musician/minister/mentor would stay alive on a heart machine. He suffered two heart attacks and congestive heart failure and now open-heart surgery. Jesus Christ was the strength for family and him.

Cure a Man of Evil Spirit (Mark 5:1-20)

An associate pastor called to help a man who was a Satan worshiper. He learned about Jesus Christ and was delivered. It is a remarkable story.

Heals Crippled Man (Mark 2:1-12)

A pastor's heart was weakened through the death of his wife. A terrible accident took place but in the situation, he glorified God and was blessed.

Personal Response

FIVE

Supernatural Passion

The Bible says, "My heart says seek him."

PSALM 27:4, 5

"One thing I ask of the Lord that I may dwell in the house of the Lord all the days of my life, to gaze upon the beauty of the Lord and to seek Him in His temple, For in the day of trouble, He will keep me safe . . . my heart says of you, seek His face! Your face Lord, I will seek" (Psalm 27:4, 5, 8). This means with intensity. In the previous verse, a strong affirmation has been recorded. "The Lord is my light and my salvation, whom shall I fear" (v.1-3). The New Testament counterpart to this is, "If God be for us, who can be against us" (Romans 8:31). My life is and will continue to be wrapped with His arms (v.4-5). I will have a sense of His protection and will not worry but music will flow into my heart (v.6).

Some people think that Jesus was just God. Others think that He was just a man, or just an angel. Some think that He was an angel and a man. *I believe that Jesus was and is God incarnate, which means that He is both God and man.* Jesus was born of a human mother (Galatians 4:4). He grew up like any other human being (Luke 2:52). He was hungry (Matthew 4:4) and thirsty (John 19:28). He grew weary and needed rest (John 4:6). He felt sadness and cried (John 11:35). He suffered (John 19:1), died (John 19:33) and was buried (John 19:40-42). He was human in every sense that we are, yet He was without sin (Hebrews 4:15).

I have discovered that He is one person who has two natures, human and divine. Jesus, God the Son, existing as the second person of the triune God, united His divine nature to a human nature, and came into the world through that. He did not stop being God when He added humanity to Himself. Remember, God has no limitations.

We are "one-dimensional beings", and He is not. In Deuteronomy 6:4, it says "Yahweh, our God; Yahweh is a plurality within an indivisible unity." God is one divine nature shared by three persons — the Father, Son, and Holy Spirit. God the Son has an infinite nature assumed in addition to a finite nature. There is one divine nature, or essence, of God. In Jesus Christ, we have added a human nature. Jesus is the Son of God (Lord) and Son of Man (Savior).

I am convinced that Jesus Christ can do whatever He wills to do according to His character. Jesus is my spiritual and physical healer. Whatever my needs are, He already knows about them. He knows how I will react or act toward them. He knows what works for me and what is best for me. My decision is simply, "Thy will be done." I have a growing passion for Jesus Christ. In my intense search, He will make me free in my need. He said, "If you remain in my word, you are truly my disciples and you will know the truth and the truth will make you free" (John 8:31, 32).

I have confidence in Him because of who He is. If I learn to do what He says to do, I will have continual assurance of His presence, power, and peace. These characteristics will be flowing through my veins because I learned to take His perspective in all things. Real hope for me is freedom and growth found in God's grace. Everything I have been writing about seems to be a mystery. It works if I gaze upon Jesus and obey His Word. The Scripture starts with "If you . . ." I must respond with my head and heart to the gospel. In my childhood, I received Jesus into my life and began a growing relationship. The Christian walk is hard and can be a struggle because the old nature is fighting against it. I have and will continue to relinquish my will to Jesus because true liberation comes when my heart says "yes" to God's words "follow me."

In my billfold, I carry a pastoral prescription card. It refreshes my mind to do certain things if I want freedom. Many things can go wrong and bring pain, confusion, worry, and struggle. My health, finances, addictions, motives, decisions, self-esteem, confidence, etc. can easily be affected. ***As I continually gaze upon Jesus, I will be set free.*** The prescription offers a Biblical solution. It is an "exchange strategy" (Philippians 4:6-9). I am learning to recite appropriate Scripture to meet my needs. His perspectives, with prayer and thanksgiving, replace mine. Reflection follows with His presence providing reason for praise and positive memories. This will lead to reliance on His promises which becomes habitual meditation. Thinking right becomes an ordinary practice. His perspective, presence, promises, and power take over in my life pattern and bring peace and a single focus. Jesus is indeed my passion.

Personal Response

SIX

Supernatural Justification

The Bible says, "Jesus was delivered for our justification and was raised for our justification."

ROMANS 4:25

"Therefore as by the offense of one judgment came upon all men to condemnation; even so by the righteousness of one the free gift came upon all men unto justification of life" (Romans 5:18). Justification means to acquit or to declare righteous. It is a legal term used for a favorable verdict in a trial. No one can withstand God's judgment (Romans 3:9-20). The law was not given to justify sinners but to expose their sin. To remedy our lost, condemned situation, God sent His Son to die for our sins in our place. When we believe in Jesus, God imputes His righteousness to us. God is both a righteous judge and the one who declares us righteous. He is our justifier (Romans 3:26).

I am justified through Christ's death. Scientific historical evidence proves that the crucifixion took place. Justification starts with a relationship with Jesus Christ. Redemption takes place when we acknowledge what God has done. Believe in your heart the truth. Salvation comes through acknowledgement, belief, and confession. Justification is through faith alone (1:16, 17; 3:24). I was standing with love and confidence in court. The judge thought I was a representative and substitute. The addicted teenager needed help, not jail. I was willing to help as a representative of the boy. I represented the church. The judge thought I was a lawyer, but I told him I was the boy's pastor, and seeking the best possible means for him. The judge wanted to meet with me after the trial. He took his robe off and shook my hand. He said he appreciated what I did for the boy and that he had many more boys and girls who needed representatives like me. He asked if I wanted to help them. This was the beginning of a new ministry for me.

Personal Response

Supernatural Resurrection

The Bible says, "These are many infallible proofs."

The God of the Bible is the true God. Christ was not made but declared the Son of God by the resurrection (Romans 1:4). Jesus Christ bases His authority of claims and teachings on His resurrection (John 2:13-22). The resurrection of Jesus Christ alone gives certainty. The resurrection is God's seal on Christ's claim to divinity.

There are "many infallible proofs" of the resurrection (Acts 1:3). The book of Matthew says that it was "very early on the first day of the week" (28:1). The book of Mark says, "It was very early on the first day of the week" (16:2). The book of Luke says that it was "at early dawn" (24:1). The book of John says, "it was still dark" (20:1). Read about these people — Matthew, Mary Magdalene, Mark, Mary the mother of James, Luke, Joanna, John, and Peter.

The sightings of Jesus on His resurrection give a solid answer to the question given to me, "Why do I believe in Jesus Christ?" Jesus Christ is my "Mighty God and Counselor" (Isaiah 9:6). He has directed me, using His people, circumstances, and decisions to guide in my life. Even in the small details, His sovereignty is experienced. My main goal in my life and studies is to know Jesus Christ. He is the foundation of all sound knowledge and learning.

Personal Response

EIGHT

Supernatural Cleansing

The Bible says, "Be reconciled to God and become righteous."

II CORINTHIANS 5:20, 21

Supernatural cleansing is the new birth. Wrap yourself around Christ. I am obtaining knowledge of God. The word 'know' is knowledge. It's not only intellectual understanding of truth but *a living participation* in the truth (I John 17:3). "This is life eternal, that they might *know* thee the only true God, and Jesus Christ . . ." I belong to Christ. I am in union with Him, I am united to Him. I am in His family. Cleansing is the process in trusting a person. Jesus Christ is the Savior (I Peter 1:11; 2:12; 3:2; 5:18). God and Savior are not two different people. Christ is God and Savior (II Peter 1:1). In order to be our Savior, He had to give His life on the cross and die for the sins of the world. When we trust Jesus Christ as our Savior, His righteousness becomes our righteousness, and we are given a right standing before God. Supernatural cleansing takes place (II Corinthians 5:21). It is a gift of God to those that believe. Grace is God's favor to the undeserving. God channels grace to us through Jesus Christ (John 1:16). God's righteousness and grace provides the experience of peace (Romans 5:11; Philippians 4:6-7). Supernatural cleansing is introduced through knowledge of the truth.

I understand that cleansing finds its authority in Jesus Christ. A response to church, service, experience, and doctrine are essential for spiritual growth, yet understanding Christ transcends them all. I have to understand who Christ is and be identified with Him in His redemptive work (John 8:12, 32). He is my source of values, our authority, and our goals. Notice these facts about Christ. They convince me and provide conviction and confidence.

- Christ was involved in the creation of the world (Col.1:16).
- Christ was totally God (I John 1:1-3).
- Christ decided to be born (Matthew 1:16).
- Christ became human without sin (I John 1:6-18).
- Christ became the spotless Lamb of God.

Supernatural cleansing has its authority in Jesus Christ.

Man is body because he possesses flesh, bones, nerves, brain, blood, and vital organs. "And the Lord God formed man of the dust of the ground (I Corinthians 15:47). Notice these facts about man and his condition:

- Man was created by God (Genesis 1:1).
- Man was created in God's image (Genesis 1:26).
- Man was born in sin (Ephesians 2:8).
- Man is dependent on God (I John 5:28).

- Man is a soul (Genesis 1:26-27).
- Man is a body (Genesis 2:7).

I believe man is a spirit because he is dependent upon God. The breath of God was an endless life not subject to death. ". . . may your spirit and body be preserved complete, without blame at the coming of our Lord Jesus Christ (I Thessalonians 5:23). God's image refers to spirit, soul, and body. "Let us make man in our image" (Genesis 1:26-27). Supernatural cleansing involves spiritual transformation.

I believe in the divine plan of God, when before the foundations of the world, He unconditionally chose those whom He would save (Romans 8:28-30; John 6:44). God's foreknowledge is more than part of His omniscience. It is a relationship established with the elect before the world began (II Timothy 2:19; I Peter 1:20). Notice these facts about salvation:

- God unconditionally chose souls to be saved (Romans 8:28-30).

- God has become a substitute
  (II Corinthians 5:21).
- God has provided redemption (I Peter 1:21).
- God is my reconciliation (I John 2:2).
- God prepared the way (John 10:28-30).
- God prepared a Christ-centered life
  (John 16:2-4).

The new birth produces an inner spiritual cleansing.

"Not by works of righteousness which we have done, but according to his mercy He saved us, by the **washing of regeneration** and **renewing of the Holy Ghost,**" (Titus 3:5). The new birth produces a living hope.

"Blessed be the God and Father of our Lord Jesus Christ, which according to his abundant mercy hath **begotten us unto a living hope,** by the resurrection of Jesus Christ from the dead," (I Peter 1:3). The new birth produces a life characterized by righteousness.

"If ye know that he is righteous ye know that **every one that doeth righteousness is born** *of him,*" (I John 2:29). The new birth produces a life characterized by freedom.

"*Whosoever is born of God doth not commit [practice] sin,* for his seed remaineth in him, and he cannot [practice] sin, because he is born of God," (I John 3:9). The new birth produces a life characterized by love.

"We know that we have passed from death unto life, because we love the brethren. He that loveth not his brother abideth in death ... Beloved, let us love one another, for love is of God and *every one that loveth is born of God and knoweth God,*" (I John 3:14; 4:7). The new birth produces a life characterized by obedience.

"For this is the love of God, that we keep his commandments, and his commandments are not grievous. *For whatsoever is born of God overcometh the world* and this is the victory that overcometh the world, even our faith," (I John 5:3-4). The new birth enables one to know and believe the truth.

"*Whosoever believeth that Jesus is the Christ is born of God*, and every one that loveth him that begat loveth him also that is begotten of him," (I John 5:1). Supernatural cleansing is secure in our believing.

Personal Response

NINE

Supernatural Action

The Bible says, "I am a doer of the word."

JAMES 1:22

Faith is a response of trust in a person, based upon that individual's character and word, which issues in action.

My Responsibility

I will move forward as I practice faith. God's plan will work as I become responsible. My responsibility is to respond to God on the basis of what is said in the Scripture. I cannot earn the grace of God. I must "hear faith" (Galatians 3:2-3). My belief is not based on rules and forms but believing and receiving the baptism of the Spirit by the "hearing of faith."

My Action

Faith is much more than an intellectual assent to a group of ideas. It is an action. The Bible says, "Remembering without ceasing your work of faith, and labor of love and patience of hope in our Lord Jesus Christ, in the sight of God and our Father" (I Thessalonians 1:3). Genuine faith is a practice. It deals with the way I live. Every day, I must make a decision to accept God's will and glorify Him. I will overcome as I love, be patient, and hope in Jesus Christ.

My Strength

My strength is nourished on the words of faith. These words refer to the basis of my faith in the Scriptures. The word of God is the very foundation for what we are to believe as well as the blueprint. In my troubled time facing ill health from head to toe, the Scripture has become my resource. Strength is provided (I Timothy 4:6). I will and have attained it. I am thankful for the Bible. It has truly been my source of strength.

My Warfare

I have been reminded that I have a fight on my hands. Since I belong to the Lord Jesus Christ, a war is going on. The devil hates the Savior and can only strike out at Him and His people. I also have a conflict with the world as well as my fleshly desires. I have to choose to praise the Word of God. I will receive divine protection (I Timothy 6:12). The Bible is powerful. It's a big exercise to see it in action. Through faith I am using His promise to obtain victory.

My Certainty

Doubt and fear will come into my presence. I have to learn that there is a union of the Scriptures and faith. There comes to pass a spiritual act whereby the promises of God and my faith are united and become one. Faith is the body of truth believed (II Timothy 4:7). Faith is the response of submission, obedience, and trust (John 1:12). There is a response of faith and the word of God united. My certainty is assured. I cannot separate the true act of believing from that which is believed.

My Relationship

Let's keep in memory that Jesus is the author and finisher of our faith (Hebrews 12:2). He has given me the gift of faith. He will sustain me. He makes it possible to enter into His presence in heaven. I live with trials, confusion, frustration, and disappointment. But with a serious attempt, I can choose genuine faith.

My Possession

I am a doer of His word (James 1:22). I possess God's precious faith (II Peter 1:1). The word 'precious' shows me the value of faith. The highest value in life is spiritual. The most priceless benefits are found in grace. I want to be characterized with faith, love, and hope. Obedience, fruitfulness, joy, and peace are included. Faith is Jesus' plan for me to succeed. Each thought will draw me closer to Him.

My Sin

The Bible tells us that all people are sinful. That's probably not what you wanted to hear! In our culture, the word sin is not often used. People don't like to think of themselves as sinful or label others as sinful. But in reality, sin is a disease that infects the entire human race. No group of people is exempt from sin. At the heart of all the troubles in the world lies sin. Where does this sin come from? If we examine the first book of the Bible we see right away that sin entered God's perfect world of creation through the deception of Satan (see Genesis 3). Satan is the enemy of God and therefore the enemy of all humans.

My Choice

The gospel is the "Good News," the news that Christ died for us and rose again for our sins. Why is the news so good? Well, the Good News makes a new person out of you. You cannot change on your own. You cannot enter heaven on your own. You cannot live a full and complete life on your own. If you respond with your mind and heart to the gospel, you will see a change in your life. I have studied different religions, human nature, and my own behavior, which has led me to realize that the gospel is the only answer to the challenges of human existence. Jesus Christ is the only way.

We have learned the facts concerning our sin, and it demands a personal response. I had to make a decision to believe what God had to say and to trust Jesus Christ as my only hope for forgiveness and eternal life (John 10:9; Acts 20:21). It has been the most important decision of my life. Have you made that choice? If not, just pray:

"Dear God, I know that I am a sinner. I believe that You sent Your Son to die on the cross to pay the penalty for my sin. I put my faith in You and trust You completely. Come into my heart and control my life. Thank You Lord."

If you prayed that prayer, you can be assured that you are now a Christian. Contact me, and I will help you grow in your new life!

Personal Response

Supernatural Faith

The Bible says, ". . . look unto Jesus the author and finisher of our faith."

HEBREWS 12:1, 2

"Let us draw near to him." The troubled heart in part will vanish when I answer the question, "How do I draw near to Jesus to prepare for heaven?" It is through accepting the exercise of faith in Jesus. I like reading God's Word. Sometimes I only read a verse or two at a time. I listen to the impression it makes upon my spirit. My soul reacts with delight and talks to God through prayer. Faith requires thinking and illumination from the Holy Spirit. I need to know the meaning of faith and how to live victoriously with it. It starts with God speaking, "let us run with patience the race that is set before us. Looking unto Jesus the author and finisher of our faith" (Hebrews 12:1, 2). The theme of Hebrews is a solemn warning against the coming short of victory and encouragement to press on in spite of all my difficulties. Faith is the challenge. I remember in my childhood I learned a broad meaning of the word faith — "forsaking all I trust him." I want to build on its meaning. Remember that willful sinning, deliberate, and continued disobedience and failure to judge known sin may result in "falling away." This results in God's judgement with only one purpose in mind – that of correction, not damnation.

I can have victory through faith. Victory implies a battle. Salvation is free, but victory means sacrifice. To win the race requires discipline. To experience victory, I have to understand faith. Conquering faith is what I am interested in. My childhood faith was easy. I took God at His Word. In the uncertainties of my adult life, I have to do the same thing. I believe the unreasonable, impossible, and inexplainable because Someone else in whom I have absolute confidence has said it was so. Upon His Word, I believe it without asking any further proof (Hebrews 11:1-3).

I accept the truth simply upon the word of someone else and without proof or any other evidence. It is believing what I cannot see, hear, feel taste, smell, or understand. It is confidence in another. Who do I trust? My belief in God is based upon the record of His Word. This is backed up by an eternity of faithfulness. No one who has ever put his trust in Him has ever been lost or disappointed (I John 5:9, 10). I think it all goes back to Genesis 1:1. The natural man wants to reason out the origin of the universe and come up with a thousand speculations. The believer rests upon the simple statement of God: "In the beginning, God created the heavens and the earth." God does not stop to explain. He is not obliged to satisfy my curiosity or stoop to satisfy my mental concerns. He is absolute, final, and true. This first verse of the Bible is the first example of faith. If I can believe that He spoke everything into existence and that He has no beginning or end, I can believe anything else He has to say. I can believe all the miracles: that He could become man and be God, that He prepared for my redemption, that His blood can cleanse me, and that He is the author of faith and its authority.

The victory of faith is won through sacrifice. It is a battle and will cause wounds, scars, and disappointments, yet in the end will be a glorious crown of victory. He requires me to surrender for service, to separate myself from the world, to abstain from sinful pleasures, and to refuse to compromise with evil (Romans 12:2).

I absolutely need to know how to grow in faith since it is the key to living eternally. How do I live victoriously on a daily basis on my route to heaven? I have learned that worship starts the faith process. I must start with the Lamb of God. The foundation is in my salvation in Jesus Christ. He is the giver of faith. He provides the direction, guidance, authority, and confidence. Religious activities are not the means. It is through my daily devotion to Him (John 4:23) and relationship development. My worship will take me from the present to eternity, and from eternity to unending life with Christ. It will become a Holy Spirit-stimulated vitality. True worship requires me to approach God with my whole person. It is a love for God in gratitude for what He has done. I have to experience an intimate relationship with God. My invisible part, or spirit, must meet with God. My entire being is activated through love (Matthew 22:37, 38). To understand faith requires God-consciousness through praying, praising, reading the Bible, thoughtful meditations, etc. Faith will grow when I make the choice to be sensitive to God's will. I have to practice the presence of God. My union with Jesus Christ will establish a reliant trust and reverent worship.

The faith process starts with worship and will continue with a walk that glorifies Jesus Christ. I have to ask myself the question, "how deep is my fellowship with Jesus?" Developing communion with Jesus Christ begins by recognizing His residence in me. At the same time, my faith will grow because the foundation is sound. The divine genius of the Scriptures, the Holy Spirit, is my indwelling helper and counselor. A change has taken place because I have made a confession of faith (Romans 10:9, 10). With that confession, the Holy Spirit dwells in me (Romans 8:9). I have a tremendous responsibility: will Christ be magnified in my body? The top priority is always to die to self. Yielding to God's will and dedication to Jesus as Lord is necessary. His indwelling presence is not in my imagination, but the real thing.

The divine transformation will take place when I answer the question, what does it mean to be Christ-centered? Jesus says give me your body and mind. I have to learn to respond to Jesus' demands. He is the dominate influence in my life. Applied Christianity is spiritual transformation. This involves sound doctrine, renewing of the mind, behavioral change, and a willing heart.

The divine transformation will lead to the divine will. God will work His will in me. He is shaping me into the image of His Son. Each day belongs to Him, and I must surrender all to Him. His will is that I understand that the mind controls the body, the will controls the mind, and the Spirit leads the way. I have to learn to just let go of self and let God do it. He will accomplish His will (Romans 12:1, 2).

The faith process involves sincere worship, a surrendered walk, and sacrificial work. My work ethic is based upon eternity. "Work for the night is coming" (John 9:4). This phrase has led the way to many projects. Faith has opened the door. When worship has the proper motivation, it will prepare me to have the correct mindset – biblical spirituality. When my walk, or behavior, is Christ-centered, it will prepare me to live out what I believe within. The faith process will be reflected in the work God has given me to do. The proclamation of the Word through music, ministry, and mentoring all have been built upon each other. It has been a joyful experience to reflect on His work being accomplished. Victorious faith will continue with a restful spirit in my life as I worship with sincerity, as I walk in surrender, and as I work sacrificially. The Old Testament heroes of faith like Abel, Enoch, and Noah will be my examples. "I will run the race with patience . . . looking upon Jesus the author and finisher of my faith" (Hebrews 2:1-3).

Personal Response

Conclusion

The answers to the question, "Why do I believe in Jesus Christ?" is found in the Word infallible as it relates to Christianity. There is no error in the Christian faith. Jesus said, "I am the way, the truth, and the life. No man cometh unto the Father but by me (John 14:6). "There is none other name under heaven, given among men, whereby we must be saved" (Acts 4:12). Christianity is based upon historical acts and facts. Believe in Jesus Christ and you will have confidence, conviction, and be convinced in the truth.